The Entrepreneurial Mindset: How to Think Like a Successful Business Owner

Written By

James "JC Edwards" Canty

Copyright © 2026 TCC Services

Dedication

For those who aspire to build something of their own, never stop taking leaps towards your entrepreneurial journey!

This book is dedicated to you!

With Love,

JC

Table Of Contents

Chapter 1: Introduction - Why the Entrepreneurial Mindset is Crucial for Success

When we think about successful entrepreneurs, we often picture their companies, their breakthroughs, or their financial success. But what truly sets them apart isn't just what they've built— it's *how they think*. The entrepreneurial mindset is the secret ingredient behind every innovative idea, recovered setback, and bold risk that pays off.

The Power of Mindset

In business—and in life—your mindset determines everything. The entrepreneurial mindset is more than confidence or creativity; it's a way of seeing the world as full of opportunity, even in uncertainty. It's about approaching problems with curiosity instead of fear, and persistence instead of panic. When you think entrepreneurially, challenges aren't roadblocks— they're training grounds for your next leap forward.

A Tale of Two Thinkers

Sara Blakely's story is a powerful example. At 27, with $5,000 in savings and zero experience in fashion, she turned frustration into innovation by creating Spanx. Every "no" she heard became fuel to refine her idea. Her success didn't come from resources—it came from resilience and creative action. That's mindset in motion.

Elon Musk shows this same principle on a different scale. Whether launching Tesla or SpaceX, he's demonstrated what happens when you think big, embrace uncertainty, and continually adapt. Musk isn't fearless—he simply chooses to act despite fear because his vision drives him more than his doubts.

But you don't need to be a billionaire or celebrity to think this way. Take a small café owner who adjusts their menu after customer feedback, or a freelance designer who reinvents their services when the market shifts. Both are practicing entrepreneurship through adaptability, creativity, and calculated risk.

You might not build rockets or clothing empires—but when you strengthen your mindset, you're already in the same league of thinkers.

Why It Matters

Every successful entrepreneur you admire shares one truth: their thoughts led them to action, and their action created opportunity. Without this mindset, talent stalls. With it, ordinary people build extraordinary things. That's why cultivating the entrepreneurial mindset isn't just helpful—it's *essential.*

Through this book, we'll explore the mental frameworks that drive success—from resilience and grit to risk management, creativity, goal-setting, and continuous learning. Each chapter will offer not just insight, but practical tools to help you embody the traits that lead to growth.

Mentor Moment

Before you dive in, take a moment to ask yourself:

- How do I react when something doesn't go as planned?

- Do I see obstacles as reasons to stop, or as chances to grow stronger?

Your answers reveal where your entrepreneurial mindset already shines—and where it's waiting to expand.

Remember, greatness doesn't start with a business plan. It starts with a belief: *You are capable of creating something remarkable.*

Chapter 2: What is the Entrepreneurial Mindset?

When we hear the word *entrepreneurship,* we often picture risk-takers, innovators, and dreamers shaping the future. But the real difference between those who succeed and those who stop short isn't luck or talent — it's mindset. The entrepreneurial mindset isn't about titles or status; it's about how you think, react, and grow in the face of uncertainty.

Seeing Opportunity Through Challenge

Entrepreneurs see problems as invitations to create solutions. They lean into uncertainty instead of retreating from it. Oprah Winfrey expressed this beautifully when she said, *"The biggest adventure you can ever take is to live the life of your dreams."* Her journey — from humble beginnings to global influence — proves that mindset expands the boundaries of what's possible when your vision outweighs your fear.

A true entrepreneurial mindset redefines failure. It understands that every setback is data, every challenge is training, and every mistake refines your direction. Whether you're starting a small business, leading a team, or launching a creative idea, how you think determines how far you'll go.

Core Traits of the Entrepreneurial Mindset

1. Creativity — Thinking Beyond the Obvious
Entrepreneurs look at the ordinary and see new possibilities. They ask, "What if?" and "Why not?" Creativity isn't luck — it's a practice of curiosity. It comes from listening deeply, observing patterns, and daring to combine ideas that others overlook. Build creative habits: take notes on inspiration, ask questions that

challenge assumptions, and give yourself permission to experiment.

→ *Reflection:*   What's a problem in your daily life or community that you could solve differently with a fresh idea?

2. Resilience — Rising After the Fall

No journey worth taking is easy. What defines entrepreneurs isn't avoiding failure, but learning from it. Resilience means accepting hardship as part of the process. It's the internal voice that says, "I'll find another way." Remember, every "no" brings you one step closer to the "yes" that matters.

→ *Reflection:*   Think of a time you faced rejection or a setback. What lesson from that experience still serves you today?

3. Calculated Risk-Taking — Courage with Strategy

Entrepreneurs are not reckless adventurers — they are informed risk-takers. They build systems to evaluate choices, measure outcomes, and act with courage when the potential reward aligns with their vision. The goal is not to eliminate fear, but to act wisely *alongside* it.

→ *Reflection:*   When was the last time fear kept you from acting? What's one small, calculated risk you could take today?

4. Adaptability — Growing Through Change

Markets shift, trends evolve, and no plan survives unchanged. Adaptability allows entrepreneurs to stay flexible, curious, and ready to pivot. It's what keeps a business alive — and a dream relevant. The most adaptable thinkers always ask, "What's this moment trying to teach me?"

→ *Reflection:* How easily do you embrace change? Could flexibility be your new competitive advantage?

5. Visionary Thinking — Seeing What Doesn't Exist Yet

Successful entrepreneurs dream beyond what's currently visible. They map the future and reverse-engineer the steps to reach it. Visionary thinking isn't about fantasy — it's clarity. It blends imagination with execution. Write your vision down, refine it often, and look at it every morning.

→ *Reflection:* What does your *bigger picture* look like? If everything went right, where would your work take you?

6. Passion — Fuel for the Journey

Passion sustains effort when motivation fades. It's the inner drive that keeps your purpose alive through obstacles. Passion grows from alignment — doing work that reflects who you are, not just what you do. Stay close to what excites you; it's the compass that keeps your energy authentic.

→ *Reflection:* What issue, idea, or mission stirs your energy no matter how difficult the work becomes?

7. Action Orientation — Turning Thought into Movement

Ideas only matter if you act on them. Entrepreneurs are doers — they don't wait for perfect conditions. They learn by moving forward and adjusting course as they go. Remember, momentum grows from motion, not perfection.

→ **Reflection:**   What small step could you take within the next 24 hours to move your idea forward?

The Cycle of a Growth Mindset

At the heart of every entrepreneurial quality is one deeper principle: *growth.* A growth mindset means believing that you can learn, adapt, and improve through effort. It rewires your perspective from "I can't" to "I can't yet."

Sir Richard Branson embodied this belief when he said, *"The amount of time people waste dwelling on failures instead of putting that energy into another project always amazes me."* His approach wasn't magic — it was momentum.

To adopt a growth mindset:

- **Embrace failure** as feedback.

- **Seek continuous learning** to stay sharp.

- **Surround yourself** with people who challenge and uplift you.

- **Reflect weekly** on lessons learned and applied.

Your Entrepreneurial Awakening

Entrepreneurship isn't limited to boardrooms or startups. It's a mindset that applies to daily life — to parenting, leading, teaching, organizing, and creating. Every time you solve a new problem, adapt to change, or reinvent your path, you're thinking like an entrepreneur.

Pause before moving to the next chapter and consider this:

Where might I already be demonstrating the entrepreneurial mindset without realizing it?

Recognizing those patterns is the first step toward owning your identity as a creator, leader, and change-maker.

Chapter 3: The Power of Mindset in Business

Business success doesn't begin with a perfect plan — it begins with perspective. The way you *think* about challenges, people, and possibilities shapes everything you create. Your mindset isn't just a quiet thought process; it's the unseen engine behind every decision, partnership, and opportunity you pursue.

Fixed vs. Growth: Two Ways of Seeing the World

Some people believe talent, intelligence, and success are fixed — that you either have it or you don't. This way of thinking limits potential. Entrepreneurs with a growth mindset know that ability can be developed. They see effort as progress, feedback as guidance, and failure as valuable information.

In business, this difference is everything.
A fixed mindset says, "I failed — therefore I'm not capable."
A growth mindset says, "I failed — therefore I learned what doesn't work yet."

The entrepreneur's superpower lies in that one word: *yet.*

Cultivating a Growth Mindset

Growth isn't an instant transformation; it's a daily discipline. You build it like a fitness routine for your mind, using challenges as resistance that strengthens you over time.

1. **Embrace Challenges** – Tough moments test commitment, not capability. Each time you push through discomfort, you expand your capacity to endure and execute.

→ **_Reflection:_** When did a situation you resisted at first become your greatest teacher?

2. **Learn from Failure** – No entrepreneur escapes setbacks. What matters is whether you extract lessons or excuses. Treat every misstep like research for your next breakthrough.

→ **_Reflection:_** What's one "failure" from your past that actually redirected you toward progress?

3. **Practice Persistence** – Consistency transforms potential into proof. Move forward even on slow days. Progress doesn't always feel dramatic — often it looks like daily discipline.

→ **_Reflection:_** What small daily action could move your business closer to its vision?

4. **Choose Your Circle Wisely** – The people around you feed or drain your mindset. Surround yourself with problem-solvers, optimists, and mentors who remind you what's possible when you doubt yourself.

→ **_Reflection:_** Who are the three people in your circle that consistently inspire growth?

The Voice in Your Head: Positive Self-Talk

Your internal dialogue determines your external results. Every business decision — from pitching an idea to handling rejection — runs through that inner voice first. When you tell yourself, "I'm capable of learning this," you invite courage. When you say, "I always mess up," you plant hesitation.

Start catching the words you say to yourself and rewriting them with intent:

- "I can't figure this out." → "I haven't figured it out *yet.*"

- "I'm not ready." → "I'm preparing to be ready."
Small shifts in language create massive changes in momentum.

Believe Before You See It

Elon Musk, Oprah Winfrey, and countless others succeeded because they believed in *their capacity* before others did. Belief is not blind optimism — it's evidence of possibility that only you can see in the beginning. Every business starts as an unseen vision in someone's mind before it ever becomes a product, service, or movement.

Think of belief as the currency of entrepreneurship: the more you invest in it, the higher the return on every action you take.

Practical Steps for Strengthening Mindset

- **Focus on Progress, Not Perfection.** Celebrate small wins. Momentum builds when you appreciate forward motion.

- **Widen Your Perspective.** Read stories of entrepreneurs outside your industry — creativity often sparks from unfamiliar territory.

- **Stay Curious.** Ask, "Why?" and "What if?" daily. Curiosity keeps your business flexible and future-minded.

- **Protect Your Energy.** Burnout clouds creativity. Schedule rest with the same importance you assign to meetings.

Gratitude: The Grounding Force

Amid hustle and high expectations, gratitude keeps ambition human. Take a moment each day to recognize what's already working — your growth, your relationships, your lessons learned. Gratitude reminds you that success doesn't begin when you "arrive." It's happening in real time.

→ *Reflection:*   What three things in your business or personal growth can you be grateful for today?

Mentor Moment

Every thriving company you admire was once an idea faced with doubt. What kept those founders steady wasn't just skill — it was faith reinforced by mindset.

You, too, can build that foundation. Don't wait for the world to validate your vision before you believe in it. Start now with the belief that progress is possible — because it is.

Chapter 4: Overcoming Fear and Failure – Developing Grit

Every entrepreneur faces fear. The fear of failing, of wasting time, of not being "enough." But what separates those who only dream from those who actually succeed is grit — the combination of courage, consistency, and belief that allows you to get back up again and again.

The Truth About Fear

Fear is your mind's way of protecting you from the unknown. It whispers doubts like, *"What if I'm not ready?"* or *"What if this doesn't work?"* But the entrepreneurial mindset doesn't silence fear — it reframes it. Fear doesn't mean *stop*; it means *prepare.* The goal isn't to be fearless; it's to move forward **with** fear riding quietly in the back seat, not steering the wheel.

→ *Reflection:*   What's one fear that's been holding you back from starting or scaling your idea? How might you take one small step through it this week?

Defining Grit

Grit is perseverance powered by purpose. It's the steady commitment to show up — especially when results come slowly. Psychologist Angela Duckworth describes grit as "passion and sustained persistence applied toward long-term achievement." Entrepreneurs live by this principle every day.

Grit isn't loud. It's built one silent decision at a time — choosing to try again after rejection, rewriting your pitch, applying for another grant, or showing up when no one's watching.

→ *Reflection:* Think of a challenge you faced that required persistence. How did staying consistent change the outcome?

Learning to Fail Forward

Failure is not the opposite of success — it's part of the journey toward it. Every successful entrepreneur can trace their breakthroughs back to moments that first looked like defeat. The difference lies in how they responded.

Instead of viewing failure as proof of inability, use it as proof of *effort.* Each closed door redirects your growth. Failure refines your vision and sharpens your resilience.

→ *Reflection:* If you could relabel a past "failure" as a lesson, which one taught you the most about yourself?

Stories of Grit in Action

Will Dean — Tough Mudder.
When Dean launched Tough Mudder, he faced financial challenges, legal clashes, and endless skepticism. But he refused to quit. His grit turned setbacks into stepping stones, transforming the obstacle-course concept into a global movement that celebrates endurance itself.

Sara Blakely — Spanx.
Blakely heard "no" dozens of times before anyone believed in her vision. Instead of shrinking, she refined her approach. Her story reminds us that rejection isn't a verdict — it's feedback.

The Everyday Person.
Think of a parent, freelancer, or community organizer who keeps showing up despite slow progress. That's grit in action — the quiet power to persist when only you can see the destination.

Five Ways to Build Your Grit Muscle

1. **Adopt a Growth Mindset.**
View effort as progress and mistakes as teachers. Replace *"I can't"* with *"I'm learning to."*

2. **Practice Self-Compassion.**
Speak to yourself as you'd speak to a friend chasing a big goal. Encouragement heals burnout faster than judgment.

3. **Break Goals Into Milestones.**
Every small win builds momentum. Progress compounds, confidence grows.

4. **Seek Mentorship and Community.**
Support transforms struggle into strategy. Find those who have walked where you're headed.

5. **Reflect and Refuel.**
Rest isn't weakness — it's preparation. Grit works best when balanced with recovery.

Resilience and Courage Combined

Resilience helps you recover. Courage pushes you forward. Together, they become momentum — the signature trait of every entrepreneur who makes the impossible achievable.

As Winston Churchill said, *"Success is not final, failure is not fatal; it is the courage to continue that counts."* That courage isn't innate — it's formed each time you choose to keep moving, to learn one more lesson, to take one more step.

Mentor Moment

You don't need to conquer fear before starting — you just need courage long enough to take the first next step. Over time, that single act of bravery compounds into strength.

Every entrepreneur you admire once stood exactly where you are, facing fear, doubt, and uncertainty. Their success didn't come from avoiding those feelings — it came from honoring them and showing up anyway.

So, pause here and remind yourself: **You've already begun.** Every page you read, every thought you rewrite, every risk you take builds the grit that will carry your vision to reality.

Chapter 5: The Power of Resiliency

Every entrepreneur, no matter how confident they appear, encounters setbacks that test their resolve. The question isn't whether challenges will come — it's how you'll respond when they do. *Resilience* is the inner strength that allows you to bend without breaking, to learn through struggle, and to rise even stronger than before.

Why Resilience Matters

Success rarely follows a straight line. There will be moments of uncertainty, rejection, and exhaustion. Resilient entrepreneurs embrace these moments as part of the process instead of proof of inadequacy. They know that pain and progress often travel together.

Resilience isn't pretending everything is fine. It's acknowledging difficulty, letting yourself feel it, and then deciding to keep moving forward. It's the steady heartbeat behind long-term success.

→ *Reflection:* When was the last time you recovered from something that could have ended your progress? What helped you bounce back?

Falling Down Seven Times, Standing Up Eight

There's wisdom in the Japanese proverb: *"Fall down seven times, stand up eight."* Each fall refines your strength. Each rise redefines your limits. The most successful entrepreneurs aren't those who never stumble — they're the ones who've mastered the art of rising quickly and intentionally.

J.K. Rowling sent her *Harry Potter* manuscript to twelve publishers before one said yes. Those rejections didn't define her; her persistence did. Her story reminds us that our resilience often writes the chapters of success long before the world notices.

→ ***Reflection:*** How might rejection or delay in your current journey actually be redirecting you toward something more aligned?

Building Your Resilience Foundation

1. **Practice Self-Care to Sustain Strength.**
Success demands energy. Protect yours through rest, balanced routine, and small moments that nourish peace.

Lesson: A calm mind makes clearer decisions.

2. **Embrace Failure as Information.**
Every misstep reveals data — what didn't work, what to refine, what to keep. Stop fearing the lesson wrapped inside the loss.

Lesson: Growth hides inside honest reflection.

3. **Find Support and Community.**
Resilient people don't walk alone. Build a network of peers, mentors, and loved ones who remind you of your "why" when pressure builds.

Lesson: Shared strength multiplies your own.

4. **Focus on Long-Term Vision.**
Temporary setbacks feel smaller when you keep a clear view of
your mission ahead.

Lesson: The big picture steadies the heart.

5. **Stay Curious and Adaptive.**
When expectations collapse, ask, "What else could this mean?"
Curiosity transforms obstacles into options.

Lesson: Adaptability is resilience in motion.

Resilience in Real Life

When Howard Schultz pushed to reinvent Starbucks as a
gathering place rather than a coffee counter, he faced resistance,
financial risk, and doubt. Yet he persisted, grounded in vision and
the belief that people deserved connection along with caffeine. His
resilience turned a simple beverage business into a global culture
of community.

Resilience shows up daily — in entrepreneurs juggling family life,
employees navigating layoffs, and dreamers rebuilding after loss.
It's less about never falling, and more about believing each fall
still belongs on your path.

→ *Reflection:* What difficult experience are you currently
reframing as preparation rather than punishment?

From Survival to Growth

Resilience starts as survival but matures into growth. At first, you recover just to keep going. Over time, you recover *wiser*. You learn to anticipate storms instead of fearing them. You begin to see setbacks not as blocks, but as breaks where strength is rebuilt.

Mentor Moment

When things feel overwhelming, return to your *why*. Purpose is resilience's anchor. Breathe, refocus, and remind yourself that every challenge is shaping the leader you're becoming.

Resiliency is the silent companion of every lasting success. It whispers, "Keep going," when everything else says, "Stop."

And as you move forward, remember this truth: you've survived every hard day so far — you are already proof that resilience works.

Chapter 6: Risk Management –
Calculated Risks and Decision Making

Every entrepreneurial journey comes with uncertainty. The question isn't whether you'll face risk — it's *how* you'll handle it. Successful entrepreneurs don't avoid risk; they manage it with insight, strategy, and confidence. They know that every bold idea needs a thoughtful plan behind it.

Understanding Risk in Entrepreneurship

Risk is not the enemy — it's an essential part of growth. Each new venture, product, or decision contains an element of uncertainty, but also potential reward. The entrepreneurial mindset views risk as a puzzle to be solved, not a wall to be feared.

Calculated risk-taking begins with awareness: understanding what's at stake, how much you can afford to lose, and what potential you stand to gain. Balance is key — bravery without strategy becomes recklessness, and caution without action leads to stagnation.

→ *Reflection:* What's one idea you've hesitated on because it felt risky? What information could help you turn that risk into a manageable step?

The Decision-Making Process

Entrepreneurs make hundreds of small and large decisions daily. The most successful ones have a system — a mental framework that reduces guesswork and increases clarity. Here's how effective decision-making usually unfolds:

1. **Gather Facts Before Feelings.**
Emotions can cloud judgment. Ground your choices in research, feedback, and measurable data.

2. **Weigh Pros and Cons Objectively.**
Write them down. Seeing trade-offs in black and white makes them easier to assess.

3. **Consider Timing.**
Even a great idea can fail if launched too soon or too late. Align your actions with readiness, not impulse.

4. **Make a Decision and Commit.**
Perfectionism kills momentum. Decide, act, and adjust if needed.

5. **Learn from the Outcome.**
Win or lose, review your process the same way athletes watch game footage — to improve the next play.

→ *Reflection:* When making important decisions, do you rely more on analysis or instinct? How could balancing both strengthen your next move?

Courage Doesn't Cancel Caution

Fear often disguises itself as logic. "I'll wait until the timing's better," it says. But waiting too long is its own risk. The art of entrepreneurship lies in calculated courage — moving despite uncertainty because your vision deserves the chance to exist.

Tom Ford once put it best: *"I'm not afraid to take a swing and miss because the home runs are going to be that much sweeter."* Real success doesn't come from always being right; it comes from daring when others hesitate.

Lessons from the Field

Debbi Fields — Mrs. Fields Cookies.
Debbi started with $50 and a passion for baking. She lacked
experience but compensated with research and relentless testing.
Each choice was a small, calculated risk — location selection,
staffing, marketing — supported by data and instinct. The payoff?
A global brand sweetened by persistence and precision.

Chip Bergh — Levi Strauss & Co.
When Bergh took over as CEO, the company was struggling. He
took decisive actions — closing underperforming stores, investing
in e-commerce, streamlining focus. Tough choices saved a legacy
brand. His lesson: leadership often means protecting the future,
not clinging to the familiar.

Everyday Entrepreneur Example.
Think about the local food-truck owner who spins a slow week
into an opportunity by adjusting their route, or the freelancer
who adds a new skill to expand client reach. These
micro-decisions, when done strategically, become the seeds of
security and scaling.

The Practices of Risk-Smart Entrepreneurs

1. **Do Your Homework.**
Research markets, customers, and competitors. Facts calm fear.

2. **Know Your Capacity.**
Identify what's truly at stake — time, money, reputation — and
how much of each you can risk comfortably.

3. **Plan for Alternatives.**
Always have a backup plan. Flexibility turns "failure" into "pivot."

4. **Start Small.**

Test before going all-in. Pilot projects provide proof before major investment.

5. **Review and Refine.**

Treat each outcome as data. What worked? What didn't? Use feedback to make your next risk smarter.

Mentor Moment

Risk will always carry uncertainty — that's what makes achievement meaningful. The goal isn't to eliminate unknowns, but to train your instincts so well that uncertainty feels less like fear and more like fuel.

The entrepreneurs who change the world aren't gamblers; they're learners. They take bold steps with their eyes open and their hearts steady.

So next time doubt arises, remind yourself: **you're not reckless for trying — you're courageous for calculating.**

Chapter 7: Creativity and Innovation – Developing New Ideas and Opportunities

At the heart of every great business is a spark — a new idea, a fresh approach, a daring solution. That spark is *creativity.* When developed intentionally, it becomes *innovation* — the process of transforming imagination into impact.

Entrepreneurs who flourish are not necessarily the smartest or most technical; they're the ones who stay curious, experiment often, and refuse to stop asking, *"What if?"*

The Creative Mindset

Creativity isn't a magical gift; it's a discipline — a way of seeing possibilities where others see limits. Entrepreneurs nurture creativity through curiosity, openness, and daily practice. Instead of waiting for inspiration, they design routines that invite it.

Start your morning with a "question sprint." Ask yourself:

- What's something my customers struggle with today?

- What's a simpler, better, or bolder way to help them?

- What if failure wasn't an option — what would I try?

By shifting from **problem-thinker** to **solution-seeker**, you train your mind to spot opportunity everywhere.

What everyday frustration could become your next opportunity if you looked at it from a fresh angle?

From Creativity to Innovation

Creativity generates ideas. Innovation turns those ideas into results. Every successful venture has walked through the same process:
Imagination → Experimentation → Implementation → Improvement.

When you combine an open mind with continual testing, you turn daydreams into deliverables. Great innovators don't aim for perfect ideas — they aim for *progress.*
Remember, the first lightbulb didn't work perfectly. But the second, the tenth, and finally the thousandth attempt changed the world.

Design Thinking: A Practical Framework

Innovative thinkers often rely on a process called *design thinking,* which blends empathy with experimentation:

1. **Empathize** — See through your customer's eyes. What do they truly need or feel?

2. **Define** — Pinpoint the exact problem to solve.

3. **Ideate** — Go wide, quantity breeds quality. Write down every idea before you judge it.

4. **Prototype** — Bring the idea to life quickly. Keep it simple and testable.

5. **Test, Learn, Refine.**

This cycle keeps momentum alive while ensuring innovation stays customer centered. Whether you're designing technology, campaigns, or art, the principles remain universal.

→ **_Reflection:_** Who are you serving with your ideas? How well do you understand their daily pain points?

Stories of Innovation in Action

Airbnb.
Built from a moment of necessity — renting air mattresses to pay rent — Airbnb reimagined "space" as connection. Their founders didn't just invent a product; they innovated how people trust one another globally.

Tesla.
Tesla fused engineering excellence with visionary design to make electric vehicles desirable, not just efficient. Their genius wasn't only in batteries — it was in rebranding sustainability as status.

Local Innovation, Global Impact.
Look around any neighborhood: a farmer using social media to sell directly, a teacher building digital courses, a stylist turning tutorials into income streams. Innovation always starts small — and close to home.

Building a Culture of Creativity

1. **Encourage Ideas without Judgment.**
The quickest way to kill innovation is to ridicule new ideas before they breathe. Postpone criticism — explore first, filter later.

2.   **Celebrate Experiments, Not Perfection.**
Reward team members (or yourself) for taking smart risks, not just for flawless execution.

3.   **Collaborate Across Differences.**
Mix disciplines, backgrounds, and perspectives. Innovation thrives where ideas collide.

4.   **Stay Inspired.**
Feed your creativity — read beyond your industry, travel, observe, and listen. Curiosity is fuel.

5.   **Document and Review.**
Keep an "Idea Journal." Date entries, revisit old thoughts, and re-examine patterns. Yesterday's note can become tomorrow's breakthrough.

Creativity as Competitive Advantage

Innovation keeps your business ahead of the curve, but it also keeps your *spirit* alive. Without it, work becomes repetition. With it, work becomes discovery. The world doesn't only need more businesses — it needs more imagination within business.

→ *Reflection:*   How can you make experimentation a regular part of your process instead of an occasional risk?

Mentor Moment

Creativity isn't something to "find." It's something to *practice.* You already have the ability — the key is permission. Permission to think boldly, to fail gracefully, and to re-imagine constantly.

Every great company began with someone saying, "Let's try." Every great entrepreneur began by answering, *"Why not?"*

You hold that power already. Protect it, practice it, and watch it open doors few others can even see.

Chapter 8: Goal Setting and Planning – Vision and Strategy

Big visions become real through clear goals and practical action. Every thriving business — from start-ups to global brands — began with someone translating a dream into a plan. *Vision* gives you direction; *strategy* keeps you on course. Combine the two, and you turn potential into measurable progress.

Start with a Clear Vision

A vision defines your North Star. It's not just what you want to achieve but *why* it matters. Clear vision answers three questions:

1. What problem do I want to solve?

2. Who do I want to impact?

3. What will success look and feel like when I get there?

Write your vision in the present tense — as if it's already happening.

"I lead a business that empowers others to grow with confidence."

This subtle shift programs your mind to act as though that future already belongs to you.

→ *Reflection:* How would your ideal version of success change not just your life — but someone else's?

Translating Vision into Goals

A dream lives in your imagination; a goal gives it instructions. Use the **SMART** framework
— *Specific, Measurable, Achievable, Relevant, Time-bound.*

- **Specific:** "Grow sales" becomes "Increase monthly sales by 15%."

- **Measurable:** Define how progress looks; data replaces guesswork.

- **Achievable:** Balance ambition with realism. Stretch, don't snap.

- **Relevant:** Align every goal with your bigger mission.

- **Time-bound:** Give every milestone a deadline to create momentum.

Nike's "Move to Zero" initiative — achieving a zero-carbon, zero-waste future — is a perfect example: a clear, measurable, time-anchored goal tied to their core values.

→ *Reflection:*   What short-term goal could you set this month that moves you one measurable step toward your long-term vision?

Create a Strategy That Serves the Vision

Strategy is your roadmap — how you'll get from intention to result. It outlines priorities, anticipates detours, and keeps your energy focused on what matters most.

Follow these steps:

1. **Assess Your Starting Point.** Know your current strengths, weaknesses, and resources.

2. **Define Milestones.** Break the journey into quarterly or monthly checkpoints.

3. **Assign Resources Wisely.** Time, money, and energy must work in harmony.

4. **Measure and Adjust.** Track, review, and refine — growth requires agility.

Airbnb's founders did this brilliantly by "growth hacking" — creating loops that turned each new user into a potential marketer. Strategy didn't stifle creativity; it amplified it.

→ *Reflection:* What small structural change could make your plan more efficient tomorrow?

Staying Agile in a Changing World

Plans require flexibility. Markets evolve, technology shifts, and unexpected events appear. Staying rigid leads to burnout; staying agile leads to innovation. Adaptability allows new opportunities to find you.

Think of Tesla pivoting production schedules or Uber shifting focus to food delivery when travel slowed. Flexibility turned risk into resilience.

→ *Reflection:* Where might flexibility make your vision easier — not harder — to achieve?

Building a Culture of Vision and Innovation

Even solo entrepreneurs build culture — every habit, response, and value creates the environment for success. Google's "20 percent time" encourages employees to explore personal projects, proving that structured freedom breeds creativity.

Encourage your team — or yourself — to dedicate time for exploration, brainstorming, and problem-solving without pressure. Innovation grows fastest in safety and trust.

Daily Habits That Support Success

- Review your goals every morning; remind yourself *why* they matter.

- Block time for your highest-value task first each day.

- Celebrate small wins — they compound into confidence.

- Journal weekly lessons learned; progress loves self-awareness.

→ *Reflection:* Which daily habit could immediately make your workday more intentional?

Mentor Moment

Your vision is the seed; your plan is the soil that nourishes it. Enthusiasm lights the spark, but discipline builds the fire that lasts.

Set your goals boldly, adjust them flexibly, and review them faithfully. Remember, it's not perfection that creates success — it's steady direction.

Every great achievement began as a clear vision written down by someone who refused to quit. Now, it's your turn.

Chapter 9: Persistence and Discipline – Building Habits for Success

In entrepreneurship — and in life — talent opens the door, but persistence keeps it open. Discipline, meanwhile, makes sure you walk through it every single day. These twin forces transform big ideas into lasting success.

Persistence is about holding the line when progress feels slow. Discipline is about showing up when motivation fades. Together, they anchor your vision in consistent action.

The Power of Consistency

Success isn't built in bursts of inspiration; it's built in rhythm — small, steady actions that compound over time. The most successful entrepreneurs share one simple trait: they keep doing the work even when no one's watching.

When motivation dips, lean on structure. Routines turn ambition into automatic momentum. Think of discipline as your personal engine — when habits take over, willpower takes a rest, and progress speeds up.

→ *Reflection:* What's one small daily commitment that, if practiced for 30 days, could transform your results?

Persistence in Practice

Persistence doesn't mean refusing to change. It means refusing to *quit.* It's the courage to keep adapting until you find the strategy that works.

Phil Knight, co-founder of Nike, faced financial struggles, supply issues, and skepticism for years before the brand found its rhythm. His story reminds us that persistence is creative — not stubborn. Each setback guided a sharper decision, each obstacle refined a better path.

→ *Reflection:*   Where might you need to persist *differently* — changing methods instead of goals?

Discipline as a Daily System

Discipline isn't punishment; it's freedom. When you create structure around your time, you leave less room for chaos and more space for growth.

Habits of Highly Disciplined Entrepreneurs:

1.   **Start the Day with Clarity and Focus.** Plan before reacting.

2.   **Prioritize the "Big One Thing."** Tackle the most impactful task first.

3.   **Track Progress.** Metrics reveal momentum — numbers tell the truth.

4.   **Minimize Distractions.** Protect your prime hours from noise.

5. **Review Evenings.** Five minutes of reflection each night primes tomorrow for improvement.

The "One Thing" principle used by Keller Williams real estate leaders echoes this truth: focusing on the single most meaningful action creates a ripple that moves everything else forward.

→ *Reflection:* Which part of your routine most needs structure — your mornings, your priorities, or your follow-through?

Persistence and Discipline Together

Persistence fuels passion. Discipline gives it direction. Passion without order burns out; order without purpose grows stale. When they unite, your effort becomes unstoppable.

Howard Schultz embodied this blend at Starbucks — committed to his vision, yet steady in practice. He persisted through rejection and showed the discipline to retrain staff, redesign stores, and never compromise quality. That mix of heart and habit turned coffee into a culture.

Turning Habits into Identity

Lasting habits stick when they reflect who you *believe you are.* Instead of saying, "I'm trying to be more consistent," say, "I'm a consistent person."
The mind aligns behavior with identity — speak your discipline into existence.

→ *Reflection:* Finish this sentence: *"A disciplined version of me would ______ every day."*

Mentor Moment

Persistence keeps your flame alive; discipline shapes how it burns.
Both are already in you — they just need attention and rhythm.

You don't have to be perfect to be consistent; you just have to show up more often than you don't. Over time, those small, ordinary efforts become extraordinary outcomes.

So today, recommit to your progress. One step. One promise. One habit at a time. **That's how successful entrepreneurs — and resilient dreamers — are made.**

Chapter 10: Continuous Learning and Adaptation – Staying Ahead of the Curve

The most successful entrepreneurs are lifelong students. They understand that learning doesn't end with a degree, a milestone, or a profit margin — it's an ongoing process that fuels growth. In a business world that evolves faster every year, the willingness to keep learning is what keeps you relevant, creative, and resilient.

The Learning Mindset

Continuous learning begins with humility — the awareness that there's always more to discover. It's about replacing "I know this" with "What else can I learn?" Every challenge becomes a classroom; every conversation holds a new insight.

In entrepreneurship, curiosity is currency. Markets change. Technology advances. Customer expectations evolve overnight. The learner's mindset transforms these shifts from threats into opportunities.

→ *Reflection:* When was the last time you learned something unexpected that improved your business or personal life?

Adaptation in Action

Adaptation is learning applied. It's the capacity to notice change early, respond quickly, and grow stronger because of it. Netflix exemplifies this principle: once a DVD-by-mail service, now a global entertainment powerhouse. Instead of resisting disruption, they became it.

Adaptation doesn't demand massive pivots every month — sometimes it's as simple as refining communication, updating your tools, or rethinking your habits. The key is flexibility powered by awareness.

→ *Reflection:* What part of your current process could become more efficient with an open mind and a small adjustment?

How to Stay Ahead of the Curve

1. **Feed Your Curiosity Daily.**
Read, listen, or watch something outside your usual topics. Innovation is often born at the intersection of disciplines.

2. **Ask for Feedback and Listen Deeply.**
Customers and colleagues are living data. Honest feedback exposes blind spots no spreadsheet can.

3. **Analyze and Update Your Metrics.**
Track performance, spot trends, and adjust strategy in real time. Insight only matters if it leads to change.

4. **Embrace New Tools and Technologies.**
From AI platforms to automation software, today's resources can s ave time and expand reach. Explore before you decide — but don't ignore them.

5. **Invest in Your Own Growth.**
Courses, workshops, mentors, conferences — these aren't expenses; they're accelerators. Growth compounds when you invest in yourself.

→ *Reflection:* What one skill, if mastered this year, would most elevate your vision or business?

Cultivating A Culture of Learning

If you lead a team, your attitude toward learning sets the tone. Encourage questions. Celebrate experimentation. Replace blame with curiosity when mistakes arise. A culture that treats learning as normal stays innovative and energized.

LinkedIn's former CEO Jeff Weiner once said, *"The skill that's going to be most valuable in the coming years is the ability to learn quickly."* That ability doesn't just sustain businesses — it sustains leaders.

Lifelong Learning as Longevity

The entrepreneurs who thrive long-term treat learning as a lifestyle. They don't just react to change; they anticipate it. They collect perspectives, mentor others, and remain students of their own industries.

Learning sharpens intuition, and intuition guides adaptation. When your mindset stays fresh, your business stays future-ready.

→ *Reflection:* How would your outcomes improve if you viewed every obstacle as a lesson first?

Mentor Moment

Stay curious, stay flexible, stay teachable. The moment you think you've learned enough is the moment progress pauses. Each lesson — even the uncomfortable ones — shapes the sharper, wiser version of you that your next opportunity requires.

Continuous learning isn't about keeping up. It's about staying inspired, evolving with purpose, and building a legacy that grows as you do.

So keep reading, asking, experimenting, and adjusting. The world belongs to those who learn fastest and apply what they discover with courage.

Chapter 11: Networking and Collaboration – Building Relationships and Partnerships

Entrepreneurship is not a solo sport; it's a community effort. The most successful people know that relationships expand potential faster than any strategy alone. Networking and collaboration aren't just career tactics — they're essential parts of an entrepreneurial lifestyle that thrives on connection, trust, and shared learning.

The Power of Relationships

Every breakthrough happens through people. A single introduction can lead to a key hire, a vital investor, or a new source of inspiration. But authentic networking is never about collecting business cards or likes online — it's about building *mutual value.*

Ask not just, *"What can I gain?"* but *"What can I give?"* When you serve first, opportunities find their way back. The most magnetic leaders are those who help others shine.

→ *Reflection:* Who in your network could benefit from your skills or insight this week? What would happen if you reached out simply to help?

Connection Over Competition

In a world obsessed with winning, collaboration defies ego. True entrepreneurs recognize that cooperation amplifies growth.

When you collaborate, you multiply strengths, distribute risk, and spark innovation that never could've existed alone.

Just look at Brian Chesky and Joe Gebbia, who built Airbnb not through isolation but through open dialogue, shared problem-solving, and a network of mentors. Their idea grew because they built *with* others, not *apart* from them.

Similarly, Quincy Jones and Lionel Richie turned creative partnership into cultural impact when they co-wrote *"We Are the World"* — a testament to the synergy of collaborative brilliance.

→ **Reflection:** Who could help you see your current idea from a new angle? Whose strengths could complement your own?

Elements of Effective Networking

1.   **Be Genuine.** Don't network just to be remembered — connect to understand. LISTEN as much as you talk.

2.   **Stay Curious.** Ask questions that reveal shared goals. People value being seen and heard.

3.   **Follow Up.** Relationships fade without nurture — send a note, share an article, or check in regularly.

4.   **Diversify Your Circle.** Grow beyond your niche. Inspiration often lives outside your comfort zone.

5.   **Give Credit.** Champion others publicly. Gratitude builds loyalty faster than self-promotion.

→ **Reflection:** How can you expand your network beyond people who think and work like you?

The Art of Collaboration

Collaborating effectively means blending creativity with humility. Every partnership works best when egos step aside and purpose takes center stage. Before starting any joint project, clarify three things together:

1. What's our shared vision?

2. How will we communicate and make decisions?

3. What does success look like for *both* of us?

Collaboration is not compromise — it's a combination. Two visions, when aligned, create something neither could on their own.

Networking in the Digital Era

Social platforms, podcasts, and virtual events have turned networking global. But even in the age of technology, authenticity still wins. The most powerful digital connections come from real curiosity and value exchange — comment thoughtfully, contribute meaningfully, and show genuine support for others' work.

Online or off, the principle remains: relationships are built at the intersection of generosity and consistency.

→ *Reflection:* What online community or event could you join this month to connect with like-minded doers?

Turning Relationships Into Partnerships

Partnerships flourish when values align. Choose collaborators whose integrity matches their ambition. Every agreement should rest on shared purpose, transparent communication, and mutual accountability. When trust leads, friction fades.

Remember — a partnership isn't just an exchange of resources; it's an exchange of belief. It says, *"We're stronger together."*

Mentor Moment

Networking opens doors; collaboration builds new rooms entirely. Treat every connection as a seed — nurture it with gratitude, authenticity, and reliability.

The people you meet today may become tomorrow's clients, partners, allies, or friends who remind you why you started.

As you grow, remember: your network is not just your net worth — it's your *support system.* And when you help others rise, you elevate yourself.

Chapter 12: Entrepreneurial Excellence – The Path to Success in Business and Life

Entrepreneurial excellence isn't about never failing — it's about never settling. It's the art of striving for mastery in both business and personal growth. True excellence means showing up every day with purpose, adapting with grace, and leading with integrity. It's not perfection; it's progress refined by perseverance.

Defining Entrepreneurial Excellence

Entrepreneurial excellence is the consistent ability to create value — not just for profit, but for people. It's building something that outlasts you because your purpose drives it more than your paycheck.

Excellence shows up in quiet habits: honoring commitments, learning from mistakes, and choosing the long view over quick wins. It's steady optimism anchored by action.

→ *Reflection:* What does excellence mean for you right now — achievement, impact, or fulfillment?

Continuous Improvement as a Lifestyle

Excellence is a moving target, always inviting you to expand your potential. Like elite athletes or artists, entrepreneurs improve by practice. They observe, evaluate, and evolve.

Mary Barra, CEO of General Motors, embodies this growth mindset. She leads with the conviction that progress requires constant learning. Her philosophy — "If you're not growing, you're dying" — mirrors the heart of entrepreneurial excellence: evolve or be outpaced.

→ *Reflection:* What routine or behavior could you fine-tune this week to raise your personal standard just 1 percent?

Purpose Over Profit

Companies like Patagonia prove that excellence doesn't compromise ethics. Founder Yvon Chouinard built a business model where purpose guides profit. From sustainable materials to social responsibility, Patagonia's success reflects alignment between values and execution.

When your *why* remains clear, decisions become easier. Excellence follows purpose, not ego. The more authentic your mission, the more meaningful your results.

→ *Reflection:* What values guide your decisions when profit and principles compete?

Collaboration and Culture of Excellence

Great leaders cultivate excellence in others. They build teams that echo their vision and empower progress from within. IDEO's collaborative design culture demonstrates how diverse minds drive innovative outcomes by valuing every voice at the table.

Entrepreneurial excellence expands when you help someone else succeed. Mentorship, feedback, and shared wins sustain the growth cycle. Excellence, after all, multiplies through connection.

→ *Reflection:* Who in your circle could you encourage or mentor this month?

Resilience and Responsibility

When challenges strike, excellent entrepreneurs respond, not react. They carry resilience like armor — forged through failure, strengthened through humility.

Patagonia's environmental initiatives and ethical stance demonstrate that excellence demands accountability. Success without responsibility isn't excellence; it's ego. True leaders use influence to uplift both people and planet.

→ *Reflection:*   How can your business or personal brand contribute beyond profit?

Mentor Moment

You already have what excellence requires: courage to start, resilience to continue, and purpose to guide you forward. Excellence doesn't require grand gestures — it thrives in daily dedication, honest reflection, and the decision to do your best even when no one's watching.

Commit to small improvements, aligned intentions, and authentic service. Excellence isn't an outcome — it's a lifestyle. Live it, and it will echo through everything you touch.

Conclusion

As we reach the end of *The Entrepreneurial Mindset*, remember: entrepreneurship is less about building a business and more about building *yourself*. The strategies within these chapters — from mindset and creativity to risk, discipline, and collaboration — are building blocks for a life designed on purpose, not by chance.

The entrepreneurial journey is rarely straight or simple. You'll face challenges, question your direction, and sometimes start again from scratch. But each obstacle is a mentor in disguise. Each setback teaches resourcefulness, humility, and determination — the very traits that define enduring success.

The habits you've cultivated — resilience, self-discipline, curiosity, adaptability, and courage — are more than business tools; they're life principles. Apply them anywhere, and you'll continue to grow, lead, and create impact.

Remember this: you don't need to have it all figured out before you begin. You just need the willingness to learn, the faith to take that first uncertain step, and the persistence to keep going once you do. Growth begins where comfort ends.

So keep pushing, keep experimenting, and keep believing in the vision only you can see. Entrepreneurship isn't a destination — it's a lifelong practice of faith, creativity, and focused action.

You already have everything you need. The mindset you've built through these pages is your blueprint for lasting success. Trust it. Refine it. Live it.

"Success is not something you chase. It's something you attract by the person you become."

Now go build boldly — your next chapter begins with you.

Acknowledgments

Thank you to everyone whose real-world inspiration helped shape the voice and lessons of this book.

I encourage other entrepreneurs to continue sharing their stories.

You never know how your journey can inspire others!

YOUR PERSONAL NOTES

YOUR PERSONAL NOTES

www.ingramcontent.com/pod-product-compliance
Lightning Source LLC
Chambersburg PA
CBHW071510130726
47997CB00006B/2474